SE...

EMPTY NEST

Time for Letting Go

Thomas D. Sauline

Little Rock
Scripture Study

A ministry of the Diocese of Little Rock
in partnership with Liturgical Press

Nihil obstat: Jerome Kodell, OSB, *Censor Librorum.*
Imprimatur: ✛ Anthony B. Taylor, Bishop of Little Rock, February 3, 2017.

Cover design by Ann Blattner. Cover photo: Thinkstock Images by Getty. Used with permission.

Photos/illustrations: Page 6, *Joseph Sold by His Brothers*, by Anna Bilinska-Bohdanowicz. Wikimedia Commons. Used with permission. Pages 9, 12, 13, 19, 24 (both), 25, 27, 30, 35, 36, 38, Thinkstock Images by Getty. Used with permission. Pages 21, 33, Lightstock. Used with permission.

Scripture texts, prefaces, introductions, footnotes, and cross-references used in this work are taken from the *New American Bible, revised edition* © 2010, 1991, 1986, 1970 Confraternity of Christian Doctrine, Washington, DC and are used by permission of the copyright owner. All Rights Reserved. No part of the *New American Bible* may be reproduced in any form without permission in writing from the copyright owner.

ISBN: 978-0-8146-3695-4 (print); 978-0-8146-3696-1 (ebook)

Contents

Introduction

Alive in the Word brings you resources to deepen your understanding of Scripture, offer meaning for your life today, and help you to pray and act in response to God's word.

Use any volume of **Alive in the Word** in the way best suited to you.

- **For individual learning and reflection,** consider this an invitation to prayerfully journal in response to the questions you find along the way. And be prepared to move from head to heart and then to action.
- **For group learning and reflection,** arrange for three sessions where you will use the material provided as the basis for faith sharing and prayer. You may ask group members to read each chapter in advance and come prepared with questions answered. In this kind of session, plan to be together for about an hour. Or, if your group prefers, read and respond to the questions together without advance preparation. With this approach, it's helpful to plan on spending more time for each group session in order to adequately work through each chapter.

- **For a parish-wide event or use within a larger group,** provide each person with a copy of this volume, and allow time during the event for quiet reading, group discussion and prayer, and then a final commitment by each person to some simple action in response to what he or she learned.

This volume is one of several volumes that explore the theme of **Seasons of Our Lives**. While the Scriptures remain constant, we have the opportunity to find within them a fresh message as we go through life facing various challenges. Whether the circumstances in our lives change due to our own decisions or due to the natural process of aging and maturing, we bring with us the actual lived experiences of this world to our prayerful reading of the Bible. This series provides an opportunity to acknowledge our own circumstances and find how God continues to work in us through changing times.

Coping with Change

Begin by asking God to assist you in your prayer and study. Then read through Genesis 37:27-36, a small but important portion of the story of Joseph and his family.

Genesis 37:27-36

²⁷"Come, let us sell him to these Ishmaelites, instead of doing away with him ourselves. After all, he is our brother, our own flesh." His brothers agreed. ²⁸Midianite traders passed by, and they pulled Joseph up out of the cistern. They sold Joseph for twenty pieces of silver to the Ishmaelites, who took him to Egypt. ²⁹When Reuben went back to the cistern and saw that Joseph was not in it, he tore his garments, ³⁰and returning to his brothers, he exclaimed: "The boy is gone! And I—where can I turn?" ³¹They took Joseph's tunic, and after slaughtering a goat, dipped the tunic in its blood. ³²Then they sent someone to bring the long ornamented tunic to their father, with the message: "We found this. See whether it is your son's tunic or not." ³³He recognized it and exclaimed: "My son's tunic! A wild beast has devoured him! Joseph has been torn to pieces!" ³⁴Then Jacob tore his garments, put sackcloth on

his loins, and mourned his son many days. [35]Though his sons and daughters tried to console him, he refused all consolation, saying, "No, I will go down mourning to my son in Sheol." Thus did his father weep for him. [36]The Midianites, meanwhile, sold Joseph in Egypt to Potiphar, an official of Pharaoh and his chief steward.

After a few moments of quiet reflection on the passage, consider the following background information provided in Setting the Scene.

Setting the Scene

The book of Genesis tells an empty nest story. The Joseph saga relates how the Israelites leave their home in the Promised Land to settle in Egypt. It all begins when the sons of Jacob plot to get rid of their brother, Joseph. His ten older brothers of another mother are jealous of him. Jacob has lavished Joseph with favors, like the gift of a fine tunic of many colors. In his musical version of this story, Andrew Lloyd Weber calls the tunic an *Amazing Technicolor Dreamcoat.* Joseph is a dreamer too.

One day, shepherding with his brothers, Joseph tells them about two of his dreams (Gen 37:5-11). In one, he dreamt that ten sheaves of wheat bowed down to his sheaf of wheat. In another, the sun and moon and stars do him homage. Recognizing themselves as the ten sheaves and the stars paying homage to their younger brother, they have had enough. So they decide to kill him.

Genesis 37:27-36 will be explored a few
verses at a time. Questions that appear
in the margins are for your personal
reflection or for discussion with others.

Understanding the Scene Itself

²⁷"Come, let us sell him to these Ishmaelites,
instead of doing away with him ourselves. After
all, he is our brother, our own flesh." His brothers agreed. ²⁸Midianite traders passed by, and
they pulled Joseph up out of the cistern. They
sold Joseph for twenty pieces of silver to the
Ishmaelites, who took him to Egypt. ²⁹When
Reuben went back to the cistern and saw that
Joseph was not in it, he tore his garments, ³⁰and
returning to his brothers, he exclaimed: "The
boy is gone! And I—where can I turn?"

Reuben convinces his brothers to dump
Joseph into an empty well. They take his cloak
for resale. Then they plan to sell him as a slave
to their regular trading partners, the Ishmaelites.
In the meantime, another group of nomads, the
Midianites, rescues Joseph from the well, takes
him to Egypt, and sells him as a house servant
to a wealthy Egyptian, Potiphar.

³¹They took Joseph's tunic, and after slaughter-
ing a goat, dipped the tunic in its blood. ³²Then
they sent someone to bring the long ornamented
tunic to their father, with the message: "We
found this. See whether it is your son's tunic or
not." ³³He recognized it and exclaimed: "My

son's tunic! A wild beast has devoured him! Joseph has been torn to pieces!" ³⁴Then Jacob tore his garments, put sackcloth on his loins, and mourned his son many days. ³⁵Though his sons and daughters tried to console him, he refused all consolation, saying, "No, I will go down mourning to my son in Sheol." Thus did his father weep for him.

When the brothers discover that Joseph is gone, they soak Joseph's tunic in blood and concoct a story. Back home, they tell Jacob that a lion attacked and killed Joseph. They show him the blood-soaked tunic as evidence. Grief-stricken, Jacob mourns the loss of his son whom he thinks is dead.

While Jacob and his wives do not have an empty house, they do have a fractured family. Their nest is emptier without Joseph. Throughout the years before they find Joseph in Egypt, the family does its best to live in the grief over their loss. They cope with the changes in the dynamics of the family. Jacob misses his favorite son. He may blame his older sons for neglecting

Do you have any regrets about the way you raised your children? If so, ask God for help to forgive yourself.

What concerns do you have for your young adult children who are out of the house? For yourself as an empty nest parent? How can trust in God's loving care help you cope with the uncertainties of the future?

to keep Joseph safe. The older brothers may feel guilty for what they did. They let their jealously cloud their judgment. They may even miss his dream stories too. Benjamin, Joseph's brother by Rachel, Jacob's favorite wife, has lost his older brother. They struggle with their loss unaware of the future reunion. Much love and care for one another probably helped them cope with the dramatic changes in their family.

Empty nest parents have a lot in common with Jacob. They love and care for their children when growing up. They have sheltered, fed, and clothed them. Many of their clothes still hang in the closet of their empty bedrooms. They sorely miss their young adult child when gone. A missing young adult child is a loss for which to grieve. Their young adult children encounter struggles over which the parents have no control. They rely on the comfort of the remaining family members to adjust to their empty nests.

36The Midianites, meanwhile, sold Joseph in Egypt to Potiphar, an official of Pharaoh and his chief steward.

Midianites rescue Joseph from the well, take him to Egypt, and sell him as a house servant to a wealthy Egyptian, Potiphar. Unknown to his family, Joseph rises to prominence in Egypt (see Gen 42–47). He comes to the attention of Pharaoh by interpreting the ruler's dreams that predict a famine. Pharaoh puts Joseph in charge of the food reserves in preparation for the famine. Years later the famine brings the brothers of

Joseph to Egypt looking for food. Eventually Joseph reveals himself as their brother. Overjoyed to have found their brother alive, they go home and bring back their father, Jacob, and the whole family. The Israelites enjoy a privileged life in Egypt until enslaved by a new pharaoh.

God accomplishes this saving work through ordinary human experiences. The Joseph story exemplifies God at work amidst the foibles, mistakes, and even sins of the human family. Joseph's jealous, conniving, and cruel brothers unwittingly become agents in God's plan. If Joseph had not gone to Egypt, the family may have died of hunger. If Joseph did not interpret dreams, he would have never come to the attention of the pharaoh. If Jacob's family had not gone to Egypt for food, they would not have been reunited with Joseph. Jacob and his family did not know what God had in store for them. Yet they trusted in God through their struggles.

The Joseph story and other patriarch sagas in the book of Genesis reveal the saving work of God. Throughout the Pentateuch, the first five books of the Bible, God continues to accomplish great things in the world through ordinary people such as Moses, Joshua, and the tribes of Israel. Genesis, Exodus, Numbers, Leviticus, and Deuteronomy tell the story of the dramatic intervention of God in human history to fulfill his promises.

The New Testament continues and magnifies the story of God's involvement in our world. A new covenant is initiated between God and God's people through the birth, death, and

Recall a family experience when things turned out better than you had anticipated. What does the experience reveal to you about God's loving care?

resurrection of his son, Jesus. The Holy Spirit acts in us, the church, and in the world as God transforms all by his loving design.

God is at work in the human family, including the family with an empty nest. This experience is common in our mobile culture. Young adult children move away to find employment. They marry and raise their families in their new locations. They leave behind empty bedrooms with beds ready for their return, personal possessions for which they have no room, graduation pictures and more hanging on the walls, and parents lonely for their company. If they marry and raise families in their new locations, parents miss the grandchildren too. Parents look forward to weekend visits when their children come home or when they travel to see their children. During these visits, hugs and conversation satisfy parents' longing for their young adult children's company. Between visits, regular contact occurs by way of phone calls, texts, Snapchats, Facebook, and other social media. Parents no longer are able to take care of them as when they were toddlers. They complain to one another about the infrequency of return phone calls and messages. So parents worry from a distance that their children are well. They pray for the well-being of their children every time they think of them.

What promise(s) did you make to yourself, your spouse, God about raising your children? How can your reliance on God help you keep these promises with your children out of the house?

Like the Israelites, parents have a covenant with God. In marriage they promise God to love and care for one another in sickness and in health until death separates them. They promise to be fruitful and multiply. God provides them what they need and the children they desire. As with slavery in Egypt and forty years in the desert, the empty nest tests these promises. Parents miss the life they had when their children were at home. They wonder why they invested so much time and treasure in raising children who are now gone. They struggle with feelings of loneliness and alienation. Yet parents know God loves them and cares for them. Their love for each other and the love of their family and friends sustain them through the challenging adjustments to an empty nest. Reassured by God's care for them up to this time in their lives, parents can be confident that God continues to care for them and their children whatever the future may bring.

Though difficult, change can transform. God's care for the Israelites transformed a cruel plot by jealous brothers into a recovery from famine. God's care for parents of an empty nest can transform the painful absence of a son or daughter into new and more loving relationships.

Praying the Word / Sacred Reading

The reflection below is provided for your time of prayer. Or you may wish to use the simple words of prayer found at the end of this section.

Families grow. Singles may become couples who marry and have children. Their children grow up and have children. The parents become grandparents. As their children and grandchildren grow, parents and grandparents grow too. Hopefully, they grow wiser and more loving. Weddings, vacations, reunions, funerals, and other occasions where these generations gather are icons of this growing family.

- Where are you in your life's journey as parents?
- Recall some joyful experiences raising your children.
- Give thanks to God for the joy your children have given you.

Families change. Jobs and houses come and go. Parents become coaches, band boosters, counselors, tutors, driving instructors, movers, and more for their children. Children become young adults. Marriages break up. Spouses die. With change comes growing pains. When parents and others look back, they often thank God for the grace to remain steadfast in their love for their families through good times and bad.

- Recall the struggles you have experienced raising your children.

- How has God helped you through difficult times?
- Talk to God about the lessons you are learning from these challenges.

Parents raise their children to be self-sufficient, mature, and loving adults. When they become adults they begin to live their own lives. Parents must now negotiate another change in the life of their family. Behavioral scientists identify this phase of a marriage as the empty nest. Eventually hatchling birds test their wings and fly out of the nest. Children grow up and leave the home. Parents are left with an empty nest. Empty nest occurs in other situations too. Some experience empty nest after the death of a spouse or anyone with whom a home was shared. Others experience it after a divorce.

- What kind of empty nest have you experienced?
- How has God helped you negotiate this significant life change?
- Offer a prayer of thanksgiving for God's grace.

Parents enjoy the benefits of an empty nest. They have less stress with a quieter house. They now have time to spend with one another, grandchildren, and friends—or on their favorite activities. Parents also cope with the losses. They miss their adult children, especially if they are out of town. They worry about their health and happiness. They have to learn news way of parenting them. They wonder about their own purpose in life now that their children are grown. Some even suffer depression.

- How has an empty nest affected you personally?
- If you are enjoying an empty nest, thank God for the blessings.
- If you are struggling with an empty nest, ask God for healing.

Parents still love their children who are out of the nest. They raised them to become mature adults. They want their children to grow up happy, healthy, and holy. When children leave home, they are doing what they are supposed to do. Parents thank God they raised them well. Parents enjoy watching their grown children use their God-given talents to make contributions in their work places and in their new communities. Parents watch with pride as their grown up children pursue intimate relationships, marry, and start families of their own.

- What gives you pride about the way you raised your children?
- Thank God for the good things your children learned from you.

You may use this prayer or one of your own making:

God, I give you thanks for the blessings of my
    spouse and my children.
I have relied on you to provide and care for
    them while raising my family.
You have never let me down. I need your help
    again.
My son/daughter has left home.
I am so proud of the young mature adult he/
    she has become.
But I miss him/her. I worry about him/her.
I am struggling to get used to an empty nest.
I pray for the grace needed to cope with the
    new changes in my life.
Because of your Son's resurrection,
I have hope that this joyful and painful tran-
    sition in my life
empowers me to love more deeply my young
    adult child.
I rely on the loving care of your Holy Spirit
    for me and for him/her.
Amen.

Living the Word

Consider how you might navigate this time of change in your life. Perhaps resolve to do one or two of the following, or make your own resolution:

- Focus intentionally on the time you are able to spend with your young adult or adult children rather than on the time when they are absent.
- Learn to offer advice to your young adult children when asked by them to do so.
- Find ways to "embrace" your grown children over long distances, making use of various technologies that could bridge the distance.
- Intentionally spend your time and attention on your spouse.

Letting Go

Begin by asking God to assist you in your prayer and study. Then read through Philippians 2:5-11, an ancient hymn that encourages us to see in Christ the model for living.

Philippians 2:5-11

5Have among yourselves the same attitude that is also yours in Christ Jesus,

   6Who, though he was in the
      form of God,
   did not regard equality with
      God something to be grasped.
   7Rather, he emptied himself,
   taking the form of a slave,
   coming in human likeness;
   and found human in appearance,
   8he humbled himself,
   becoming obedient to death, even death on a cross.
9Because of this, God greatly exalted him
   and bestowed on him the name
   that is above every name,
   10that at the name of Jesus
   every knee should bend, of those in heaven and on earth
      and under the earth,

**¹¹and every tongue confess that
Jesus Christ is Lord,
to the glory of God the Father.**

*Following a few minutes of quiet reflection
on the passage above, consider the
information provided in Setting the Scene.*

Setting the Scene

Paul, the author of the letter to the Philippians, borrows an early Christian hymn about the incarnation to urge his readers to imitate the humility of Christ. Jesus, the Son of God, is born among us a servant of God's love. Jesus sanctifies our experiences of letting go in his letting go.

Life is a process of letting go. Toddlers let go of their parents' hands to walk. Preschoolers let go of their toys for bookbags. Teenagers let go of the handlebars of their bikes for the steering wheel. Young adults let go of their independence to marry. Parents let go of their time, energy, and resources for their children. Parents let go of young adult children for their children's sake. Seniors let go of favorite activities for the sake of their own health and safety. Those near death let go of their lives and place them into the hands of a merciful God.

Empty nest is a moment in this lifelong process of letting go. Parents of young adults let go of more than their children when they leave home. They may let go of furniture, appliances, cars, and money. They let go of the daily responsibilities of childcare. They let go of ways of relating to their children when living at home. They let go of all the times they spent with their children playing at home, going on vacations, traveling to soccer games, watching TV, celebrating birthdays, reading bedtime stories, watching school plays and concerts, visiting colleges, and more. Parents let go of old ways of parenting for new ways.

> *We will consider the above passage from Paul's letter to the Philippians a few verses at a time, taking time to respond to the questions found in the margins. You may be in a group discussing these questions with others, or you may want to use the questions for reflection or journaling.*

Understanding the Scene Itself

[5]**Have among yourselves the same attitude that is also yours in Christ Jesus,** [6]**who, though he was in the form of God, did not regard equality with God something to be grasped.** [7]**Rather, he emptied himself, taking the form of a slave, coming in human likeness; and found human in appearance,**

In the incarnation, Christ lets go of the glory of his divinity to become human. He emptied himself to become one of us. He gave of his divine self and fully accepted the

humanity given to him. From his birth, he experienced the love of his parents, the joy of a wedding feast, the friendship of his disciples, hatred from enemies, kindness from strangers, and other human experiences. In the crucifixion, Jesus experienced the pain of rejection, hatred from enemies, abandonment by his friends, agony of suffering, the loneliness of death, and resignation to God. In Jesus, God loves us so much that God lives with us, eats with us, cares with us, struggles with us, suffers with us, and dies with us. God shares his life with us completely. In the resurrection, God restores his divine glory in heaven and on earth. In Christ, we see God face-to-face.

Why do you suppose that the humanity of Jesus is sometimes hard for us to fathom?

Jesus lets go of the glory of his divinity. He is a model of self-giving. Jesus did not hold tight to God's glory like a child gripping a toy he refuses to share with a friend. Rather Jesus let go and accepted the human condition. He gives of himself in service to the love of God. He gives his life for the human family. Like a parent he loves without conditions. Paul admonishes his readers that they must be humble like Jesus. He wants his readers to let go of whatever holds back their love. He wants them to give of themselves in love for others.

In his *Daily Online Meditation* (July 22, 2016), Richard Rohr, OFM, reflects on the self-giving that is essential for Christian maturity. He observes that the saints are holy because they knew how much they depended on God's mercy. They knew that even the loving things they did were not perfect. They may have done them partly for selfish motives. So they gave themselves over completely to God's mercy. They became humble like Jesus. Their attitude was that of Christ. Emptied of themselves, they were open to the in-pouring of God's love. Overflowing with God's love, they generously shared it with others.

How is God calling you to give of yourself as a parent in an empty nest? What loving self-sacrifices are you making for your young adult children?

[8]he humbled himself, becoming obedient to death, even death on a cross.

This hymn in the second chapter of Philippians acknowledges the humility of Jesus who, though divine, took the form of a slave. Like a slave, Jesus became a loving servant for others on God's behalf. He literally gave his life in service to others. He healed the sick, fed the hungry, taught in parables, dined with undesirables, forgave the sinful, and died on the cross in loving service.

Christians follow the example of the humble service of Jesus by putting God and others first. They give of themselves to care for those in need of food, clothing, shelter, moral support, companionship, comfort in grief, and more. Jesus exemplified this service by washing the feet of his disciples at the Last Supper. Parents serve their children like this. They set aside whatever they are doing to respond to the needs of their children. A parent stops cooking dinner to listen to a child's troubles at school. Another parent rushes home from work to attend to a child sent home from school sick. Parents regularly forego their needs to care for those of their children. Parenting is Christian discipleship.

Empty nest parents are servants for God too. When their children lived at home, they healed a bruised knee with a bandage and a kiss. They made meals every day for their hungry children and endured undesirable behavior at the dinner table. They taught, in word and deed, lessons of love and faith to impressionable children. They forgave a child who threw a temper tantrum. After their children have gone, they continue to serve them but in different ways. Over the phone, they comfort an out-of-town son grieving over the death of a beloved pet. They bear patiently with a son- or daughter-in-law who has grown to see the world differently. They make their children's favorite meals when home for a college break. They forgive a young adult child who struggles with an addiction. Empty nest parents continue to serve their children in new and different ways.

What lessons in loving service have you learned? How are these lessons shaping your family even as it changes?

Empty nest parents struggle to imitate the humility of Jesus. They want to have the attitude of Christ. They want to be good parents. They love their children. They want their sons or daughters to live their own lives. Letting go is hard. They have to get used to an empty house. They worry when their out-of-town children get sick. They lose patience that their children are not getting their lives together. They fret about their children's car insurance, healthcare, and student loans. They don't want their children to be lonely. They wish their single children had a significant other. They disagree with how their children are raising their grandchildren. They question their children's job choices. They make their children feel guilty for not visiting often enough. They complain that their children do not return their phone calls. Letting go requires humility.

Empty nest parents also practice humility by acknowledging that they are no longer in charge of their young adult children. They can no longer insist they do what they are told. They can no longer physically remove their children from harm's way. Parents must let go of the control of their young adult children. They raised them to be independent, thoughtful, and mature adults who can think for and take care of themselves. When their young adult children leave home, parents entrust

How well are you imitating the humility of Jesus as an empty nest parent? In what ways is your attitude like that of Christ? In what areas do you hope to grow more Christlike in this regard?

their children to God. They realize that they were never really in charge. When they were raising their families, God loved and supported them and their children. When their children leave home, God continues to love and support them and their young adult children wherever they go. God is in charge, not them.

Dying to self is at the heart of Christian discipleship. Dying to self is loving others as much and maybe even more than loving oneself. Dying to self is being humble enough to realize that you are not the center of the universe. Dying to self is growing from selfishness to selflessness.

Empty nest parents die to themselves as their young adult children leave home. They die to the kind of parents they have been in order to become the parents they may be as they move forward. They have to learn how to offer loving support at long distances. When their son or daughter is sick, they offer medical advice over the phone. When their child is in harm's way of a destructive storm, they rely on God for their child's protection. When their child develops a new intimate relationship, they hope and pray their child will not get hurt or be hurtful. When there is a family event, parents have to coordinate schedules, provide overnight accommodations, and otherwise negotiate with their young adult children. Empty nest parents let go of parenting children and embrace parenting young adults.

What have you lost in your relationships with your young adult children? What have you gained?

> Empty nest parents die to themselves as they learn these new ways to support their children.

Parents are an important part of their children's lives. Their children rely on them. Parents of young children are important to their children in ways different than parents of young adults. Young children rely on their parents for all their physical needs. Young adults who have left home do not rely on their parents for these essentials. Empty nest parents may feel less valuable to their children than before, but young adult children still rely on their parents. They want their parents to support them in different ways, through their love, wisdom, and presence in good times and bad.

9Because of this, God greatly exalted him and bestowed on him the name that is above every name, 10that at the name of Jesus every knee should bend, of those in heaven and on earth and under the earth, 11and every tongue confess that Jesus Christ is Lord, to the glory of God the Father.

> Jesus taught his disciples that they must lose their lives to gain them anew. His resurrection confirms God's promise that those who die to themselves will be born to new life. Dying to old ways of parenting is difficult. As young adults

live their own lives, parents can feel unappreciated for all they have done. Empty nest parenting has its rewards as well. To the pleasant surprise of empty nest parents, their young adult children sometimes express profound appreciation to them. At Halloween, a young adult son living in another city missed the decorations and other festivities of celebrating this holiday when growing up. He realized all the efforts his parents made to celebrate Halloween and other holidays. He called his parents to tell them how glad he was to have them as parents. The painful struggles of parenting young adults can become great joys. Empty nest parents die to parenting children, and they live to parent the mature and loving young adults whom they have nurtured.

How have your young adult children given you new life?

Praying the Word / Sacred Reading

How has God blessed your relationships with your young adult children? What graces do you need to adapt to the changes in your relationships?

- Thank God for the blessings.
- Ask God for help letting go of old ways of parenting.

God, I thank you for the grace to have raised my child into a mature and loving young adult. I am struggling to let my son or daughter go. The house feels so empty. I am uncertain how to love him or her now. I am weary of making more changes in my life. I know dying to old ways of parenting can bring new joy in my relationship with my son or daughter. I pray my attitude may be more like that of your Son, Jesus. I ask for your help to grow in humility. I rely on the Holy Spirit to bring me from the death of old ways of parenting to life in new ways of parenting the young adult son or daughter that I love. Amen.

Living the Word

The hymn Paul shares in Philippians 2:5-11 praises Christ who dies to self and is then exalted.

- In your own family situation, where can you see the need to die a little more so that new life may come? Be deliberate about your focus, looking for opportunities to set aside your own agenda for the sake of a family member.
- Plan a celebration with your spouse or close friends to mark the transition from full house to empty nest. Prepare a prayer that includes the hymn from Philippians, and ask Christ to help you rise to new life.

Loving Anew

Begin by asking God to assist you in your prayer and study. Then read John 14:23-29, a scene from the Last Supper where Jesus bids farewell to his disciples.

John 14:23-29

²³Jesus answered and said to him, "Whoever loves me will keep my word, and my Father will love him, and we will come to him and make our dwelling with him. ²⁴Whoever does not love me does not keep my words; yet the word you hear is not mine but that of the Father who sent me.

²⁵"I have told you this while I am with you. ²⁶The Advocate, the Holy Spirit that the Father will send in my name—he will

teach you everything and remind you of all that [I] told you. ²⁷Peace I leave with you; my peace I give to you. Not as the world gives do I give it to you. Do not let your hearts be troubled or afraid. ²⁸You heard me tell you, 'I am going away and I will come back to you.' If you loved me, you would rejoice that I am going to the Father; for the Father is greater than I. ²⁹And now I have told you this before it happens, so that when it happens you may believe."

> *Setting the Scene offers background information to help you as you move into your reflection.*

Setting the Scene

This scene from the Gospel of John takes place at the Last Supper, after Jesus washed the feet of his disciples, after warning of Judas's betrayal, after giving the command to love one another, and after predicting Peter's denial. Now it is time for Jesus to prepare his followers for his own departure.

Parents get a lot of practice saying goodbye in large and small ways. New parents say goodbye to their infant when the baby begins to walk. Parents of a toddler send their child out to play. Parents walk their child to his or her first day of school. Parents help their child pack for a school field trip. Parents attend their child's graduation. Parents of a college graduate learn of their child's first job. They say goodbye to their college graduate leaving for a first job. Young adults wave goodbye to their empty nest parents who have come for a visit. Empty nest parents say goodbye to the child they knew.

With each goodbye, however, is a new hello. Parents celebrate the first steps of their toddler. They proudly watch their youngsters playing with the children next door. They look forward to the stories about field trips. They throw a party for their high school graduate. They thank God when their young adult gets a job. They congratulate themselves for raising a mature young adult now living independently. Each transition is bittersweet. They miss the child they knew, but they also welcome the child whom they are getting to know.

With each transition, parents learn anew how to love their children. Each life transition demands new ways of loving.

> When you left home, what did you learn about your parents and their capacity to love and support you in new ways?

The passage is considered in the following pages a few verses at a time with commentary and a few questions for reflection and/or discussion.

Understanding the Scene Itself

[27]Peace I leave with you; my peace I give to you. Not as the world gives do I give it to you. Do not let your hearts be troubled or afraid. [28]You heard me tell you, 'I am going away and I will come back to you.' If you loved me, you would rejoice that I am going to the Father; for the Father is greater than I.

Jesus says goodbye to his disciples at the Last Supper. He knows that those opposed to him want to kill him. If he is not able to return to Galilee with them after the Passover in Jerusalem, he wants to reassure his disciples of his love for them. Jesus does not want them to be afraid. He asks them to trust God will take care of him and of them. His peace he gives to them on his farewell. Jesus promises them the Advocate, the Holy Spirit, who will look after them as God has done for him throughout his public ministry. He continues to share God's love for them even after he is gone.

Jesus knows that no matter what happens his love for them will endure. After the Supper, the authorities arrest, convict, and crucify him. He dies on the cross. On the first day of the week, God raises Jesus from the dead. The risen Lord appears to his disciples again, giving them the peace of God and gifting them with the Holy Spirit to guide them as promised. Through the Holy Spirit, the risen Lord continues to love his disciples. God never stops loving them.

Empty nest parents never stop loving their young adult children even though they are out of the house. They love them differently than when they were children playing in the backyard. They must now learn how to love their young adult children at long distances. Empty nest parents cherish every visit. They support their children with texts,

What worries do you have for your young adult children? How does your faith reassure that they will be alright?

phone calls, and social media. They patiently wait for news from their children. They lovingly reassure their children who struggle at their work or in their relationships. They trust God to protect their young adult children when traveling. They hope for fulfilling intimate relationships that may lead to marriage and children. They wish their children all the best.

Empty nest parents are much like Jesus at the Last Supper. They are concerned about how their young adult children will fare without them. They want their young adult children to know how much they love them. Throughout the pain and suffering of letting go, they still wish peace for them. They trust their love for their children will empower them to love others. They know God will take care of them away from the parents and families that love them. They believe their love for them will endure even beyond the grave. By the power of the Holy Spirit, they never stop loving their young adult children.

[26]**The Advocate, the Holy Spirit that the Father will send in my name—he will teach you everything and remind you of all that [I] told you. [27]Peace I leave with you; my peace I give to you. Not as the world gives do I give it to you. Do not let your hearts be troubled or afraid. [28]You heard me tell you, 'I am going away and I will come back to you.' If you loved me, you would rejoice that I am going to the Father; for the Father is greater than I. [29]And now I have told you this before it happens, so that when it happens you may believe.**

Jesus accompanied his disciples throughout Galilee teaching them and others about the reign of God. He accompanied them on their trip with him to Jerusalem for the Passover. He had supper with them the day before he was crucified. During this Last Supper he reassured them that he would never stop loving them and that God would never abandon them. Many of them, of course, abandoned him during his arrest, trial, and execution. But Jesus never abandoned them. Even from the cross he continued to care for them. The Gospel of John recounts how Jesus entrusted his mother, Mary, to his Beloved Disciple (John 19:25-27). The risen Lord accompanied his disciples in the Upper Room where Thomas touched his wounds (John 20:24-28) and at the shore of the Sea of Galilee when he cooked them breakfast after a miraculous catch of fish (John 21:1-14). The Holy Spirit that he promised them at the Last Supper accompanied Peter, Paul, and the early church as they preached the Good News of Jesus Christ. His Holy Spirit accompanies us now in Word, sacrament, and one another, the church.

In what ways do you experience the Spirit's presence as you consider the changing relationship with your young adult children?

Inspired by the example of Jesus, Pope Francis writes about the church's ministry of accompaniment. Writing about care for those in troubled marriages in his apostolic letter *Amoris Laetitia* (The Joy of Love), he urges the church to "accompany with attention and care its most fragile children, marked by love, hurt and bewildered, restoring trust and hope, as the beacon light of a port or a torch carried in the midst of people to enlighten those who have lost their route or are in the midst of the storm" (*Amoris Laetitia*, 313).

Parents have been accompanying their children since they were born. They accompanied them home from the hospital. They accompanied them in their first steps. They accompanied them to the doctor's office. They accompanied them on the first day of school. After their young adult children leave home, they continue to accompany them.

Whether moving furniture into a new apartment, offering a wedding toast, or baby-sitting grandchildren, empty nest parents still accompany their young adult children. Alive in Christ after death, parents continue to accompany their children. Their love for their adult children lives on in the love the family shares at holiday meals, in the love their children share with their parish families and local communities, and in the love their young adult children have for those in need.

As Pope Francis urges the church, empty nest parents accompany their young adult children in love especially when they are hurt, bewildered, or lost. Although empty nest parents cannot always physically accompany their struggling young adult children, their loving care accompanies their children wherever they are, in good times and bad. Empty nest parents reassure a son on the phone who cannot get a job, text a daughter about a recent diagnosis of cancer, and pray for a son struggling with an addiction. Empty nest parents send an email sympathy card when an in-law dies. Empty nest parents are calm in the life storms of their young adults by their unconditional love for their sons and daughters. Although they may not always acknowledge their parents' loving care, young adults rely on their support. While they want to and have to deal with their crises on their own terms, young adults know that they can count on their parents' loving care. They know that their parents are still accompanying them on their life journeys.

What challenges you most as you learn new ways to accompany grown children?

In his ministry of accompaniment, Jesus loved others as they needed to be loved. In the Gospel of John, Jesus saved a bride and groom from embarrassment by miraculously providing more wine at the wedding feast (John 2:1-12). At a well in Samaria, he spoke to a woman shunned for living with a man (John 4:4-48). He saved the life of a woman caught in adultery and forgave her (John 8:1-11). At the Last Supper, he shared bread with Judas, who was about to betray him (John 13:21-30). After the resurrection, he appeared to his disciples as they hid from the

authorities, and he calmed their fears. He showed Thomas the wounds in his hands and feet. He sent the Holy Spirit to love and care for them. Jesus continues to accompany the church in ever new ways of healing, forgiving, and loving.

Parents grow in new ways of loving their children and have been doing so all along, from infancy through their school years at home. Empty nest parents balance their desire to protect their young adults with their respect for their autonomy. A house empty of children is an invitation and a challenge for parents in loving anew. Empty nest parents strive to love like Jesus in this new phase of caring for their families.

How do you accompany in love your young adult children who are out of the house? What does it mean to you that Jesus accompanies you in an empty nest?

Praying the Word / Sacred Reading

Empty nest parents learn from Jesus at the Last Supper how to bid farewell to their young adult children. With each goodbye they reassure themselves and their young adult children that all will be well. As Jesus accompanies the church through the Holy Spirit, empty nest parents accompany their adult children by sharing in the "joys and the hopes, the griefs and the anxieties" (*Gaudium et Spes*, Pastoral Constitution on the Church in the Modern World, 1).

- In what practical ways do you show your love for your children in their transitions to young adulthood?
- Thank God for the good things still in store for your young adult children and for you.

Insert the name of your young adult child or children in the blank spaces of the prayer below:

God, I thank you for the gift of ____.
I am so proud of the independence I see in
    ____, and I want the best for him/her.
I struggle with letting ____ go and wish we
    could see each other more often.
I still want to be part of his/her life.
I want to follow the example of your Son,
    Jesus,
who never stops loving us.
Sustain me in my love for ____, no matter
    what.
Help me discern how to love ____ in new and
    different ways.
Grant me the strength to support ____ in good
    times and in bad
and to look for signs of new life always.
    Amen.

Living the Word

Spend some time thinking about this phase of your life as a parent.

- List all of the "new" things that have emerged in you as you let go of your son or daughter.

- Make another list of the new life that you see in your son or daughter who has left home.
- To what extent is this journey from a full house to an empty nest an opportunity to grow closer to God in new ways?

Find or make an opportunity to share some of your experience with another empty nester.